AUTUMN
COLORING BOOK

MW00897441

Thank you for choosing Ava Browne Coloring Books.
We strive to publish unique coloring books for all ages.

If you found this coloring book enjoyable, please leave us a review.
Reviews help drive sales which allows us to make more coloring books.

Thank you and happy coloring!

www.avabrowne.com

COLOR TEST PAGE

COLOR TEST PAGE

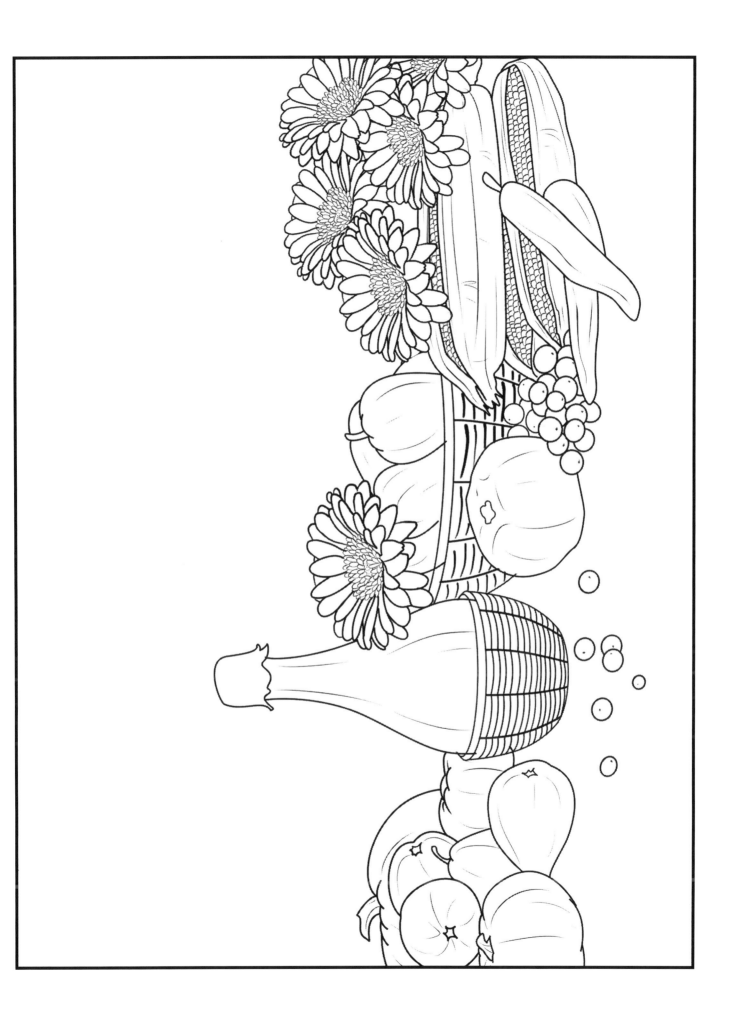

Please visit
https://avabrowne.com/autumn-download/
to download your free digital copy.
Enter the password
e6phxws3
To access the file. (all lowercase)

Made in United States
Orlando, FL
16 December 2024

55528714R00037